What the Bible Says to Abuse Survivors and Those Who Hurt Them

....

Victor Vieth

New
Growth
Press

newgrowthpress.com

New Growth Press, Greensboro, NC 27404
www.newgrowthpress.com

Cover Design: Trish Mahoney, themahoney.com

ISBN 978-1-945270-62-8 (Print)
ISBN 978-1-945270-63-5 (eBook)

Library of Congress Cataloging-in-Publication Data

Names: Vieth, Victor, author.
Title: What the Bible says to abuse survivors and those who hurt them / Victor Vieth.
Description: Greensboro, NC : New Growth Press, 2017.
Identifiers: LCCN 2017038756| ISBN 9781945270628 (single) | ISBN 9781945270642 (5-pk)
Subjects: LCSH: Adult child sexual abuse victims--Religious life. | Sexual abuse victims--Religious life. | Sex crimes--Religious aspects--Christianity.
Classification: LCC BV4596.A25 V54 2017 | DDC 261.8/3272--dc23
LC record available at https://lccn.loc.gov/2017038756

Printed in India

26 25 24 23   4 5 6 7

Pastors and church personnel often struggle to apply intentional and appropriate doses of both biblical grace and stringent accountability to victims and perpetrators of child sexual abuse. Partly as a result of ignorance, Christians often apply a heavy dosage of law (conviction) to victims and gospel (grace) to offenders. This misguided, sometimes cruel use of theological principles often drives victims away from the church and their personal walk with God and emboldens offenders to remain in their sin, and even to commit such an offense again. This book encourages a deeper understanding of both abuser and victim dynamics so that church leaders can move past ignorance and myth and tackle this devastating issue with the power of grace and truth afforded by the good news of Jesus. Here we will consider the proper biblical response to each party, as well as offer practical suggestions to assist the church in responding to both.

Overview of the Dynamics of Child Sexual Abuse

In order to spiritually counsel or assist sexually abused children in any way, churches need to understand the dynamics of abuse. Unfortunately, many have accepted decades-old myths about child sexual abuse victims, including the most harmful and prevalent: that children's allegations of abuse are inherently suspect. This skepticism toward claims of sexual abuse has led churches to focus heavily (and almost exclusively) on problematic behaviors exhibited by the child—behaviors that, ironically, may be attributable to the abuse. There is no excuse for the body of Christ to apply such a distorted view of blame and culpability to child abuse victims.

Historic skepticism toward victims of child sexual abuse

"The history of psychology in the past one hundred years has been filled with theories that deny sexual abuse occurs, that discounts the responsibility of the offender, that blame the mother and/or child when it does occur, and that minimize the impact."[1] This damaging trend, coupled with high-profile day care cases from the 1980s in which many believed children were coached into false allegations[2] spilled over into our mainstream culture, including churches. For example, one Christian publisher printed a book claiming there was an "industry" of child protection professionals manufacturing allegations of abuse to "snatch" children away from parents.[3]

Although we all need to be mindful of the possibility of false allegations, multiple studies conclude that these instances are rare[4] and that when children do lie, it is usually done to protect the perpetrator, not to get anyone in trouble.[5] Indeed, false allegations are not only a statistically remote possibility but especially rare in comparison with actual prevalence of child sex abuse—1 in 4 girls and 1 in 6 boys are sexually abused by the age of 18.[6] Law enforcement and other professionals have made great strides in conducting abuse investigations over the past 25 years, improving their skills in interviewing victimized children and collecting evidence—further reducing the risk of false allegations. **Accordingly, it is irresponsible for any pastor to automatically dismiss an abuse allegation, even against a respected member of the church.** The church is responsible for protecting the children in the church body, and this sacred stewardship is reinforced by Christ himself (Mark 10:13–16). Familiarity with the dynamics of abuse will prevent such a dangerous response.

The Child Sexual Abuse Accommodation Syndrome (CSAAS)

In order to understand the difficult, sensitive nature of how and when child sexual abuse is typically reported, consider Dr. Roland Summit's work detailing the Child Sexual Abuse Accommodation Syndrome (CSAAS).[7] This study identified the dynamics present in child sexual abuse cases that constrain children from disclosing abuse early, if at all. These dynamics include secrecy, helplessness, entrapment and accommodation, delayed, conflicting and unconvincing disclosure, and retraction.

Secrecy

Three dynamics tend to impress secrecy on the victim: 1) The private nature of sexual abuse, which can suggest the child's need to keep quiet. 2) Fear of retaliation by the abuser or ostracism by the church community. 3) A promise of protection or special privileges from the offender.

Helplessness

Child sexual abuse victims typically feel helpless to stop the abuse for reasons of powerlessness, confusion, and adult authority concepts. Their smaller size and their lack of maturity may render them feeling incapable of stopping the offense. Secondly, churches teach children to obey those in positions of authority as an act of obedience to God, and perpetrators can be good at exploiting this dynamic. They will use this teaching to admonish children to honor requests to submit to sexual conduct. Third, most sexual abuse is committed by a trusted, even loved adult, and often offenders will threaten that they will no longer love the child if abuse is revealed.

Entrapment and accommodation

Since the child victim has a secret he or she feels helpless to do anything about, Summit postulates they must often "accept the situation and survive."[8] A child may develop a coping mechanism such as convincing themselves that the sexual abuse prevents others from being victimized. Another survival strategy the child may use is disassociation during abusive episodes, subconsciously sending his or her mind to another place during abuse in order to find a "temporary emotional escape from the horror, fear, and pain."[9]

Delayed and unconvincing disclosure

Due to the dynamics above, many children never disclose sexual abuse. When children do disclose an offense against them, the report is often delayed and comes out in an unconvincing manner, due to years of stifled rage and trauma. Without awareness of child sexual abuse dynamics, the pastor may quickly dismiss the allegations without reporting the case to the authorities.

Retraction

According to Summit, "in the chaotic aftermath of disclosure, the child discovers that the bedrock fears and threats underlying the secrecy are true."[10] In other words, the perpetrator's claim the child would be isolated, not believed, removed from the home, bullied at school, or any number of other horrors does, in fact, often occur. Consequently, the child concludes that living with the lie is easier than telling the truth and recants her allegation.

A number of studies of sexual abuse victims have found that recantation is not unusual.[11] Again, clergy and laity unfamiliar with these dynamics are not only at risk to accept a recantation at face value, they are often used by perpetrators to apply pressure on children in the hope of securing a recantation. In more than one instance, for example, a non-offending caretaker has taken a child to a pastor to "confess" the lie. Church leaders would do well to take to heart the detrimental message that they are sending to their weakest and most vulnerable members when they do not rise up to better defend children.

The ACE Studies: The Medical and Mental Health Risks of Child Abuse

The Adverse Childhood Experience Study (ACE), an ongoing collaborative research project of over 17,000 adult patients studies adverse childhood experiences including abuse, neglect and witnessing domestic violence. It "reveals staggering proof of the health, social, and economic risks that result from childhood trauma."[12] Adults suffering from one or more adverse childhood experiences were statistically more likely to suffer from a variety of medical and mental health problems, and the risk increases markedly based on the number and severity of adverse experiences.

Without this knowledge, churches are at risk to dismiss an allegation of abuse and focus primarily on the victim's behaviors, including delinquent and criminal behaviors, without fully recognizing that this troubling conduct can actually be a consequence of the abuse. In spiritual terms, the danger is that a church will be quick to offer judgment for visible sin, without an appreciation of the need to provide a burdened victim with the enormous comfort of the gospel.

Spiritual injuries resulting from sexual abuse

There are a number of studies documenting the impact of abuse on spirituality. For example, a study of 527 victims of child abuse found a significant "spiritual injury" such as feelings of guilt, anger, grief, despair, doubt, fear of death, and belief that God is unfair.[13]

This spiritual impact is even more pronounced when the perpetrator is a member of the clergy. Clergy abusers often use their religion to justify or excuse their sexual abuse of children in a manner that irreparably damages their understanding of the Lord and faith matters. Specifically, church attendance of these survivors decreases, they are less likely to trust God, and their relationship with God often ceases to grow.

Some researchers have found that a victim's "spiritual coping behavior" may play either a positive or negative role in the survivor's ability to cope with the abuse. Victims of severe abuse may remain "stuck" in their spiritual development, remaining angry with God. Children abused at younger ages are "less likely to turn to God and others for spiritual support." Nonetheless, even victims describing a difficult relationship with God "still rely on their spirituality for healing." Victims who experience "greater resolution" are able to "actively turn to their spirituality to cope . . . rather than attempt to cope on their own."[14]

These findings underscore the tremendous importance of church bodies in responding properly to the victims within their congregations. If church leaders and members can provide a safe environment wherein the victim feels heard, accepted, and supported, it can restore the broken faith and tremendous spiritual injury the victim has suffered. The manner in which a congregation represents Jesus to the victim will be a lynchpin in determining their future spiritual condition.

Overview of Dynamics of Child Molesters

In addition to the need to proactively demonstrate the grace and healing of the gospel to victims of child sexual abuse, churches need to be better equipped to respond to abusers with a great degree of informed scrutiny and proactive discipline. This starts with better understanding the typical dynamics of abuse.

Not all child molesters are the same

Church leaders in most jurisdictions have a legal duty to report suspected child abuse immediately to the appropriate outside authorities, not to conduct an internal investigation or seek to confirm the suspicion. Church personnel and lay counselors are not equipped to diagnose the myriad types of sex offenders nor understand the mindset of those who sexually abuse children. And many pastors and laity assume that everyone who sexually violates a child does so for the same reason or requires the same degree of supervision, consequences, or treatment.

Having said this, there are some general characteristics of child molesters that every pastor should know—partly because sex offenders often count on clergy and laity to be ignorant. In commenting on various reasons offenders molest children, one sex offender treatment provider notes:

> There is a subgroup of child molesters who molest children simply because they are sexually

attracted to them. There are others who molest because they are antisocial or even psychopathic and simply feel entitled. There are still others who use children for the intimacy they are too timid or impaired to obtain from adults. And there are others who molest children for reasons we don't understand at all.[15]

Many child molesters are religious, and religious sex offenders may be the most dangerous

Clergy and laity can and should be cognizant of a number of pertinent characteristics of those who offend against children. For starters, sex offenders are often religious and many of them attend church. In a study of 3,952 male sex offenders, 93% of these perpetrators described themselves as "religious."[16]

There is evidence that "religious" sex offenders may be the most dangerous. One study found that sex offenders maintaining significant involvement with religious institutions "had more sexual offense convictions, more victims, and younger victims."[17]

Child molesters manipulate both children and the church

Child molesters within congregations are extremely manipulative, not only of their victims, but also the church as a whole. In the words of one convicted child molester:

> I consider church people easy to fool . . . they have a trust that comes from being Christians. . . . They tend to be better folks all around.

And they seem to want to believe in the good
that exists in all people. . . . And because of that,
you can easily convince.[18]

Child molesters are skilled at deception because, in
part, they have considerable practice at lying to everyone around them and to themselves. Not only are child
molesters skilled at lying, they are often proud of their
abilities to fool the pastors and congregants. In the
words of one convicted child molester:

There was a great amount of pride. *Well, I pulled
this one off again.* There were times when little
old ladies would pat me on the back and say,
"You're one of the best young men that I have
ever known." I would think back and think, *If
you really knew me, you wouldn't think that.*[19]

Many child molesters offend with others present

Supervision is not enough. In many instances, a
child molester offends with other children or even
another adult present.[20] According to one study, 54.9
percent of child molesters offended when another child
was present and 23.9 percent offended when another
was adult present. The abuse, of course, may be subtle
and not easily detected. For example, a child molester
in a Christian school may call a pupil up to his desk
ostensibly to review an examination while, at the same
time, touches the child's genitals which are covered from
the other students by the desk. As another example, a
father may touch the child beneath the bed covers while
his wife is asleep in the same bed. Offenders report that
molesting a child with others present may be more

arousing and may also give them more power over the child—conveying to the victim that he or she can be abused at any time, in any place, with anyone present.

The fact that many sex offenders molest victims with others present is critical for clergy and laity to understand. Offenders often argue that a child's allegations are absurd—after all, who would sexually touch a child with others in the room? An informed pastor will tell a suspect that, as it turns out, many sex offenders engage in precisely this conduct.

Many child molesters carefully select their victims

Many child molesters put a great deal of time and thought into selecting the children they will violate for two reasons. First, they are looking for the easiest target. Second, they often look for the child or children least likely to be believed should he or she disclose. A church member convicted of sexually abusing children at church describes this in chilling detail:

> First of all you start the grooming process from day one . . . the children that you're interested in. You find a child you might be attracted to. . . . For me, it might be nobody fat. It had to be a you know, a nice looking child. . . . You maybe look at a kid that doesn't have a father image at home, or a father that cares about them . . . if you've got a group of 25 kids, you might find 9 that are appealing . . . then you start looking at their family backgrounds. You find out all you can . . . which ones are the most accessible . . . you get it down to one that is the easiest target, and that's the one you do.

Simply stated, child molesters often select damaged children or, in the alternative, they damage the children and then cite the damage as proof the victim cannot be believed.[21]

Child molesters often twist concepts of sin and guilt

Child molesters often use religious or spiritual themes in the abuse of children. Child molesters may cite a child's biological reaction to abuse and contend the victim equally enjoyed the abuse and is equally sinful. It is not uncommon for a molester to pray with his victim and ask God's forgiveness for both.

Sexual abuse in the name of God creates a "triple trauma" involving the abuse itself, the betrayal of trust, and spiritual harm that often includes threats regarding God and damnation, as well as the incitement of fear and confusion.

A teenage victim of a neighborhood child molester told me, as the prosecutor preparing her for court, that she had not disclosed the abuse for years because she was certain her church would reprimand her for the sin and not the offender. The child had so internalized the perpetrator's messages that she saw no difference between sinning and being the victim of sin.

Law & gospel

In distinguishing between law and gospel, Martin Luther described the terms this way:

> The gospel is the message about the incarnate Son of God, who was given us without our merits for salvation and peace. It is the word of salvation, the Word of grace, the Word of comfort, the Word of

joy. . . . But the Law is the Word of perdition, the Word of wrath, the Word of sadness, the Word of pain, the voice of the Judge and the accused, the Word of unrest, the Word of malediction.[22]

Although Luther's description of law and gospel is clear, the great reformer acknowledged the complexity of applying these concepts to individual cases. Indeed, Luther said that anyone who could accurately and consistently apply these concepts was worthy of the title "Doctor of Holy Scripture."[23] According to one theologian, "You are not rightly distinguishing Law and Gospel in the Word of God if you preach the Law to those who are already in terror on account of their sins or the Gospel to those who are living securely in their sins."[24]

Applying Law and Gospel to Victims of Child Sexual Abuse

With all this in mind, a church seeking to properly apply the whole counsel of Scripture to victims of child abuse will likely find a clear course of action—the liberal use of the gospel, and the sparing use of the law. To this end, the following guidelines may be helpful.

Avoid the temptation to focus on the victim's sins

A pastor meeting with anyone abused as a child may see the exploitation's aftermath—a child or adult who has turned to alcohol, drugs, smoking, sex, food, or a thousand other worldly attractions in search of solace. In the face of such behaviors, they may also be the subject of church gossip and consequently feel completely alone. One may be tempted to focus on their outward sinful behavior and away from the gaping hole

in the child's heart—an injury that can only be filled by
the gospel. A pastor succumbing to the temptation to
judge may lose the child forever—and will one day be
subject to the gaze of a Savior who asks us to care for
the suffering and promises to hold us accountable for
our failure to love those rejected by the world.

Instead, recognize the brokenness they may have
displayed for years. Jesus came to bind the wounds
of the broken hearted and the gospel may be the only
tonic the abused child has never experienced. The pastor must pour out this oil liberally.

Assure the victim of Christ's empathy

A victim may struggle to believe the very nature and
character of God. One psychologist describes the prob-
lem this way: "The sexual violation of a child can have
many spiritual effects. A distorted image of God coupled with a distorted image of the self creates several
barriers to experiencing God's love and grace. . . . God
is often perceived to be punitive, an impossible task-
master, capricious, impotent, indifferent, or dead."[25]

A Christian pastor or leader must show the child a
very different image of God. They must tell the victim
that those who abused him or her violated the clear com-
mandments of God. Any twisted theology employed in
justification came not from God, but from Satan himself. Christian leaders then must tell them that Jesus
understands such toxic theology—after all, the devil
employed that trickery on Christ as well (see, for example, Matthew 4:1–11). Speak of Christ's love of children
and the grave warnings he gave to anyone who harms
them—telling his disciples that the angels of children
have direct access to his Father and that it is better to be

tossed into a sea with a millstone around their neck than to hurt a child (Matthew 18:6). Tell them that Christ, the very Son of God, was a descendant of a sexually exploited woman (Joshua 2; 6:22–25; Hebrews 11:31; Matthew 1:5), and was frequently seen in the company of other sexually exploited women as he promised not only his help, but the very kingdom of God (Matthew 21:31). Also remind them that he is the Suffering Servant who came to bear our sorrows (Isaiah 53:4).

Refrain from platitudes

Well-meaning Christians can be quick to offer a biblical platitude to these complex spiritual struggles. When this happens, a victim often feels frustrated, misunderstood, and their trauma oversimplified. Consider, for example, the complex theological questions contained in this survivor's account of trauma:

> When I was a little girl, my dad would come into my bedroom to tuck me in. He would read me a story and then he would have me utter my bedtime prayers. After the prayers, Dad would sexually abuse me. When the abuse was done he would tell me things like "God doesn't hear your prayers. If he did, he wouldn't allow me to touch you sexually right after your prayers. Either there is no God or, if God exists, he is unable to protect you." I have never forgotten what my dad said. I'm a grown woman now and, every time I pray, I remember all the times I asked God to watch over me during the night, and how the prayers went unanswered. I want to pray, I want to be close to God, but I don't know how. Please tell me what to do. (Used by permission)

A pastor engaged with this parishioner will need to explore the toxic theology presented by her father as well as the difficult questions posed about prayer—a platitude won't do. Long-term counseling needs to include a series of theological discussions and other resources on these myriad issues. The pastor must be invested for the long haul.

Assist in accessing appropriate medical and mental health care

The victim may be living with extreme guilt over the usage of drugs or alcohol, failed relationships, or a host of other problems. Recognize the enormity of this pain and assure the survivor of God's forgiveness and love. Simply stated, the pastor must display the compassion of our Savior. The church must be fully invested in walking alongside the victim, but also recognize its limitations. In providing much-needed referrals to mental health services, pastors should seek a skilled, experienced professional current on the literature addressing childhood trauma. Many well-educated counselors and therapists have had little training on child sexual abuse and thus it is critical to investigate before making a referral. In some cases, an incompetent counselor is worse than no counselor at all.

Don't make forgiveness into a law but a change of heart rooted in the gospel

Many victims of abuse struggle with the issue of forgiveness and, when forgiveness does occur, it often takes time. Consider, for example, the pain of this victim:

> I am a Christian. I have faithfully attended church all my life. I am, though, deeply

troubled. When I was a boy, my father cruelly abused me. One of his favorite things to do was to take me into the barn, strip me naked, bind my hands together with a rope and then toss the other end of the same rope over the rafters in the barn so that I would hang naked in the barn as he beat me with a stick. The sound of that stick, the smell of that barn, and the sight of my blood are never far from my memory. I am a good person, and I believe Jesus is my savior. At the same time, though, I know I'm going to hell. I recall the lesson of Jesus scolding Peter that our obligation is not to forgive seven times but seventy times seven—an infinite number of times. I recall Jesus saying that if we can't forgive others, we won't be forgiven. Try as I might, I cannot forgive my father. Why should I have to go to hell because I can't forgive the man who tortured me? (Used by permission)

This survivor has multiple theological questions that need careful consideration and compassionate responses. As a starting point, though, three concepts may be helpful. First, assure the survivor that forgiveness is not a toleration of sin. The child abuse victim has every right to have a perpetrator prosecuted and otherwise held accountable for crimes committed.

Second, recognize that forgiveness cannot be forced. Instead, suggest to the victim that forgiveness is a gift of God that allows the survivor to let go overwhelming feelings of anxiety, hatred, and anger. Many victims have said that until they forgave an offender, the perpetrator continued to have power over them.

Third, point the victim to the cross and trust the Holy Spirit to do his work. Christian psychologist Diane Langberg puts it this way:

> It has been my experience in my work with survivors that rather than simply telling them they need to forgive—a statement that often overwhelms them with despair—it is much more helpful to teach them, as they are ready, about the work of God in Christ on the cross. . . . Over time, clients see evidence of that work in their own lives. . . . The recognition of that wonderful redemption almost always results in a hunger to be like the one who has loved them so faithfully.[26]

Applying Law and Gospel to Perpetrators of Child Sexual Abuse

Avoid cheap grace

The concept of "cheap grace" is a term coined by Dietrich Bonhoeffer and is defined as "grace sold on the market like cheapjacks' wares."[27] Many sex offenders have found the value of "cheap grace" in faith communities—they have found there can be quick resolution if they cry readily and use the language of repentance, without ever taking action to rectify the damage they have inflicted. When this happens, many offenders return home, realize how easy it is to be pardoned, and will molest again. Additionally, while repentance is an important part of ministering to an offender, there are immediate and lasting consequences to this sin. For example, ministering to the offender does not preempt the legal and moral requirement to report this crime to all appropriate authorities. Also, a repentant offender must be prepared that restoration will never result in the offender being allowed unsupervised contact and access to children.

Ask tough questions and apply the law as an act of genuine love

The church should be a ready resource for continuing to shepherd a genuinely repentant wrongdoer. Part of this process will involve implementing appropriate legal and personal consequences. Ask questions like the ones below to determine the seriousness of the offender's repentance.

- If the offender has abused his or her own child:
  - Have you informed your spouse that you have sexually abused your child? If your wife wants you to move out of the house, are you willing to do it? If the child victim wants you to leave the house, are you willing to do it? Have you informed your child's medical provider that you have violated her body?
  - Have you referred your child to a counselor to assist in coping with the abuse you have inflicted on him or her?

- If an offender has abused children in the church, as opposed to in his or her own home:
  - Are you willing to inform the church body and all parents of your past? If the church body decides to remove you from corporate worship, are you willing to accept the church's decision?

- Questions for any offender:
  - Do you hold yourself fully responsible for your conduct—or do you believe your victim in some way contributed to the abuse?
  - Have you turned yourself in to the police? If the government files charges for crimes you have committed, will you plead guilty or will you force your child victim to testify publicly and be grilled by an attorney you hire?
  - Are you willing to enroll in a sex offender treatment program?

An offender who is confessing sexual misconduct but is unwilling to address the physical or emotional needs of his victim, to disclose the abuse to his spouse, or to seek sex offender treatment may be seeking forgiveness but has no intention to repair the damage inflicted or to reform his behavior.

Applying the law to an abuser in this way is a genuine act of love. A sex offender unwilling to accept full responsibility for his conduct, who continues to minimize his offense or to blame others for his conduct is not yet the "crushed" sinner ready for the gospel.

Recognize the value of earthly consequences

As a result of his actions, the offender may lose his freedom, his family, and be forever ostracized. It is only in this brokenness, though, that they will find the true power of the gospel. When sex offenders complain of prison sentences and registration requirements, remind them of the thief on the cross who accepted governmental punishments for his crimes and asked only for the mercy of God (Luke 23:41–42). It was this genuine repentance, a turning away from sin that did not seek relief from its consequences, that Jesus responded to with unmerited grace.

Conclusion

When clergy and laity apply the law to victims and the gospel to perpetrators of child sexual abuse, perpetrators are emboldened to strike again, and children are lost to the church. This is a bane on the name of Christ and on all he accomplished for us on the cross. With a large and growing body of research documenting the reality of what can happen under its own watch, the church cannot hide behind ignorance. Rather, congregations must properly apply the robust, fully-orbed gospel to victims and offenders and to otherwise fully prepare for the day of judgment when our Lord will ask each of us, "Where are the children?"

Endnotes

[1] Anna C. Salter, *Predators, Pedophiles, Rapists, and Other Sex Offenders: Who They Are, How They Operate, and How We Can Protect Ourselves and Our Children* (New York: Basic Books, 2003), 42.

[2] See, for a review, David Hechler, *The Battle and the Backlash: The Child Sexual Abuse War* (Lanham, MD: Lexington Books, 1987).

[3] Mary Pride, *The Child Abuse Industry: Outrageous Facts About Child Abuse & Everyday Rebellions Against a System that Threatens Every North American Family* (Wheaton, IL: Crossway, 1986).

[4] R. K. Oates, D. P. H. Jones, D. Denson, A. Sirotnak, N. Gary, & R. D. Krugman (2000). "Erroneous concerns about child sexual abuse." *Child Abuse & Neglect*, 24(1); 149–57.

[5] L. Lawson & M. Chaffin (1992). "False negatives in sexual abuse interviews." *Journal of Interpersonal Violence* 7, 532–42.

[6] Centers for Disease Control and Prevention. (2005). *Adverse Childhood Experiences Study: Data and Statistics.* Atlanta, GA: Centers for Disease Control and Prevention, National Center for Injury Prevention and Control. Retrieved January 12, 2009 from: http://www.cdc.gov/nccd-php/ace/prevalence.htm.

[7] R. C. Summit (1983). "The child sexual abuse accommodation syndrome." *Child Abuse and Neglect* 7, 177–93.

[8] Ibid.

[9] Herschel Walker, *Breaking Free: My Life with Dissociative Identity Disorder* (New York: Touchstone, 2009), 16.

[10] Summit, "The child sexual abuse accommodation syndrome," 188.

[11] T. Sorenson & B. Snow (1991). "How children tell: The process of disclosure in child sexual abuse." *Child Welfare* 70(1), 3, 15.

[12] Vincent J. Felitti and Robert R. Anda, "The Adverse Childhood Experiences (ACE) Study," *American Journal of Preventive Medicine* 14, no. 4 (1998): 245–58.

[13] Ronald Lawson, Charles Drebing, Gary Berg, Aime Vincellette, Walter Penk, "The Long Term Impact of Child Abuse on Religious Behavior and Spirituality in Men," *Child Abuse and Neglect* 22:5 (1998), 369–80.

[14] Terry Lynn Gall, "Spirituality and Coping with Life Stress Among Adult Survivors of Childhood Sexual Abuse," *Child Abuse and Neglect*, Vol 30 (7) 2006.

[15] Salter, *Predators*, 75.

[16] "The Abel and Harlow Child Molestation Prevention Study" (2002), http://www.childmolestationprevention.org/pdfs/study.pdf.

[17] Donna Eshuys and Stephen Smallbone, "Religious Affiliations among Adult Sexual Offenders," *Sexual Abuse: A Journal of Research and Treatment* 18, no. 3 (July 2006): 279–88.

[18] Salter, *Predators*, 29.

[19] Ibid., 199.

[20] R. C. Underwood, P. C. Patch, G. G. Cappelletty, R. W. Wolfe (1999). "Do sexual offenders molest when other persons are present? A preliminary investigation." *Sexual Abuse: A Journal of Research and Treatment* 11, 243–47.

[21] Salter, *Predators*, 57.

[22] Ewald M. Plass, *What Luther Says* (St. Louis: Concordia, 1959), 732.

[23] Scot A. Kinnaman and Laura L. Lane, *Lutheranism 101* (St. Louis: Concordia, 2010), 129.

[24] C. F. W. Walther, *The Proper Distinction Between Law and Gospel*, ed. W.H.T. Dau (St. Louis: Concordia Publishing House, 1929; 1986), 101.

[25] Diane Langberg, *Counseling Survivors of Sexual Abuse*, (Maitland, FL: Xulon Press, 2003), 91.

[26] Ibid., 185.

[27] Dietrich Bonhoeffer, *The Cost of Discipleship* (New York: Touchstone, 1995), 43.